Beautiful
WORD
BIBLE STUDIES

Ephesians
HEAD HELD HIGH

STUDY GUIDE · SIX SESSIONS

LORI WILHITE

Harper*Christian*
Resources

HarperChristian Resources

Beautiful Word: Ephesians Study Guide
© 2021 by Lori Wilhite

This title is also available as a HarperChristian Resources ebook.
Visit www.zondervan.com/ebooks.

Requests for information should be addressed to:
HarperChristian Resources, *Grand Rapids, Michigan 49530.*

ISBN 978-0-310-13094-9 (softcover)

ISBN 978-0-310-13095-6 (ebook)

All Scripture quotations, unless otherwise indicated, are taken from the Holy
Bible, New International Version®, NIV®. Copyright © 1973, 1978, 1984, 2011 by
Biblica, Inc.® Used by permission. All rights reserved worldwide.

Cover design: Ron Huizinga

Interior design: CrosslinCreative.net

First Printing March 2021 / Printed in the United States of America

CONTENTS

Beautiful Word Bible Study Series Introduction 5

How to Use this Guide 7

SESSION 1 : Chosen 9

SESSION 2 : Alive in Christ 27

SESSION 3 : Empowered by Prayer 45

SESSION 4 : Live Worthy 63

SESSION 5 : Walk in Light 81

SESSION 6 : Take Your Stand 99

Scripture Memory Cards 117

About the Author 121

WELCOME

Ephesians

HEAD HELD HIGH

SOMETIMES the Bible can seem overwhelming. Where do you go for words of comfort when you're feeling lost or frustrated in life? What book of the Bible do you turn to for wisdom about the situation you find yourself in?

The Beautiful Word Bible Study series makes the Bible come alive in such a way that you know where to turn no matter where you find yourself on your spiritual journey.

Paul, the author of Ephesians, is famed for persecuting Christians at every turn, until he had a life-changing encounter on the road to Damascus (Acts 9). His encounter with Christ transformed everything.

He became a staunch builder of the church who set off on multiple journeys to share the good news of Jesus. On his second missionary expedition he founded the church of Ephesus (Acts 18:19) and later spent two years teaching in the robust, wealthy province (Acts 19:8-10). He was eventually driven from the riotous city by fiery silversmiths who were angered by all the money they lost from Paul's teachings against worshiping false gods.

Written around 60 AD, Paul pens this letter from prison. It calls us to walk with our heads held high. There are many burdens in life that can leave us bent, stooped down, staring at the ground. It might be the burden of criticism that stirs your deepest insecurities. Or the heaviness of a struggling marriage. Or the strain of finances. Or the millstone of discouragement and darkness you can't escape. Or the crushing pain from your kiddos who are crumbling under the pressure of schools, friends, and busy schedules. And for those who are parents, we know we're only as happy as our saddest child.

Paul's letter teaches us that we don't have to live under the crushing weight of heartache and disappointment. He gives us beautiful insight into the Lord's redemptive work, and how a life that's been completely changed can change the world.

The book of Ephesians reveals that in light of what God has done, is doing, and will continue to do. You can walk confidently—shoulders back, chin up, and head held high.

HOW TO USE THIS GUIDE

Group Size

The Beautiful Word *Ephesians* video curriculum is designed to be experienced on your own, or in a group setting such as a Bible study, small group, or during a weekend retreat. After watching each video session, you and the members of your group will participate in a time of discussion and reflection on what you're learning. If you have a larger group (more than twelve people), consider breaking up into smaller groups during the discussion time.

Materials needed

Each participant should have their own study guide which includes streaming video access found on the inside front cover, video outline notes, group discussion questions, a personal study section, Beautiful Word coloring pages, and Scripture memory cards to deepen learning between sessions.

Timing

The timing notations—for example, 20 minutes—indicate the actual length of the video segments and the suggested times for each activity or discussion. Within your allotted time, you may not get to all the discussion questions. Remember that the *quantity* of questions addressed isn't as important as the *quality* of the discussion.

Facilitation

Each group should appoint a facilitator who is responsible for starting the video and keeping track of time during the activities and discussion. Facilitators may also read questions aloud, monitor discussions, prompt participants to respond, and ensure that everyone has the opportunity to participate.

Opening Group Activity

Depending on the amount of time you have to meet and the resources available, you'll want to begin the session with the group activity. You will find these activities on the group page that begins each session. The interactive icebreaker is designed to be a catalyst for group engagement and help participants move toward the ideas explored in the video teaching. The leader will want to read ahead to the following week's activity to see what will be needed and how participants may be able to contribute by bringing supplies or refreshments.

— CHOSEN —

Ephesians

Opening Group Activity [10-15 MINUTES]

What you'll need:

▶ Sheet of blank paper for each person

▶ Pens, markers, and/or watercolors

1. Each participant is invited to use the paper and drawing/writing tools to create a picture (words or images) of someone whose head is held high, one who is held somewhat up, and someone whose head is weighed down by life.

2. Discuss the following questions:

   ● Overall in your life, which picture best describes you right now? Why?

   ● Which pictures best describes you right now in the following areas of life: professional, emotional, and spiritual?

   ● What's the area of your life where you most need God to help you walk with your head held high?

Session One Video [20 MINUTES]

NOTES: *As you watch, take notes on anything that stands out to you.*

 It's time to walk with your head held high. This means that you walk with confidence and strength in who God created you to be.

 Want to walk with your head held high? Embracing that you are chosen changes everything.

What caught your attention? What surprised you? What made you reflect? Wha

Paul declares that you are chosen, adopted, and God's possession.

 Adoption in the ancient world often meant adopting adult children. If a wealthy family did not have a male heir, they would adopt a son in his twenties or thirties who would inherit the estate.

 The Romans weren't apt to adopt infants who were untarnished by life, unaffected by circumstances.

 In ancient times, when a debt was paid, the creditor wrote "Paid in full" or "It is finished" across the certificate of debt, meaning the debt was cancelled.

EPHESIANS 1

Group Discussion Questions [30-45 MINUTES]

1. Lori begins by sharing some of the burdens of life we carry. What's the one life burden that's weighing you down the most right now?

2. Read Ephesians 1:3-10. Which of the words or phrases in this passage do you struggle to believe is true of you? Which words or phrases in this passage are the easiest for you to embrace and live out?

3. Lori teaches,

> "We are **chosen** before the creation of the world, **predestined** for adoption, and **chosen** according to His plan and the purpose of His will. The idea of being **chosen** should lead us to our knees in thankfulness, to pour out our praise, to freely give our gratitude."

Describe a time when you were chosen. How did that make you feel and affect your ability to walk with your head held high? Why do you think it's easy to forget these Biblical truths in everyday life? What can you do to remind yourself?

4. Read Ephesians 1:11-14. What are some of the spiritual blessings you have in Christ? Which is most meaningful to you today?

5. Lori teaches,

"When the adoption was complete, the person who had been adopted had all the rights of a legitimate son in his new family. In the eyes of the law, he was a new person. The debts and obligations connected with his previous family were abolished as if they had never existed."

In what ways have you experienced Christ making you new? In what areas are you still clinging to your old life? Where do you most need to write the words "Paid in full" and "It is finished"?

6. What does it mean to you that the same power that raised Jesus from the dead lives in you (Ephesians 1:19-20)? What are some practical things you can do to walk with your head held high this week?

Close in Prayer

Consider the following prompts as you pray together for:

► Heightened awareness of the riches of your spiritual blessings

► Help to stay focused on the reality that you are chosen by God

► Opportunities to help others walk with their heads held high

Embracing that you're chosen changes everything.

Preparation

To prepare for the next group session:

1. Read Ephesians 2.

2. Tackle the three days of the Session One Personal Study.

3. Memorize this week's passage using the Beautiful Word Scripture memory coloring page. As a bonus, look up the Scripture memory passage in different translations and take note of the variations.

4. If you've agreed to bring something for the next session's Opening Group Activity, get it ready.

"For he chose us in him before the creation of the world to be holy and blameless in his sight."

—Ephesians 1:4

PERSONAL
STUDY TIME

DIGGING INTO THE

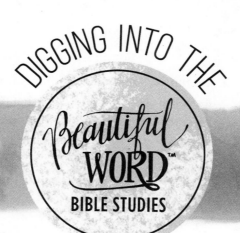

Beautiful WORD™

BIBLE STUDIES

Ephesians
CHOSEN

Some ancient manuscripts contain a blank space instead of the words

"in Ephesus."

Some scholars believe this letter was like a group text message, meant to be shared with many congregations in different cities.

DAY 1
Ephesians 1:1–2

Like many of the letters in the New Testament, Ephesians was meant to be read aloud to listeners. The tone and flow of Paul's writing often sounds more like a sermon than a literary piece. The opening verse identifies Paul as the author of Ephesians. He's described as an apostle, in the Greek *apostolos*, meaning "one who is sent with a commission."

1. Read Ephesians 1:1. Who is Paul an apostle of? Who is Paul sent by? Who is Paul sent to?

2. On the continuum below, how often do you think of yourself as being sent by God to a particular person or into a particular situation? How does remembering that God is at work in you empower you to be courageous?

I don't think of myself as sent by God to share the love of Jesus.

I know I'm sent by God to share Jesus' love everywhere I go.

After addressing the recipients of the letter, Paul delivers a greeting that often appears at the beginning of his epistles: grace and peace (v. 2). This greeting appears in thirteen letters throughout the New Testament.

3. Read Ephesians 1:2. What is the source of all grace and peace?

4. Where do you most need to experience grace and peace right now?

Some scholars note that this opening greeting echoes elements of a blessing spoken by Aaron in the Old Testament.

5. Read Numbers 6:24-26. Where are the elements of grace and peace mentioned?

6. Who in your life are you struggling to extend grace to right now; struggling to feel peace in the friendship? Write their names in the space below.

....

....

....

....

Some scholars note that **Grace** (charis) is the unmerited favor of God that's founded in his steadfast love. **Peace** (shalom) is a holistic deep wellness and completeness.

7. Take a moment to pray the Aaronic blessing of Numbers 6:24-26 over them. What practical steps can you take to show grace and peace to them this week?

DAY 2
Ephesians 1:3-14

Written in the form of a hymn of praise, Paul now offers rich thanksgiving for our bountiful spiritual blessings in Christ. The blessings relate to the past (v. 4), the present (v. 7), and the future (v. 10). It's worth noting that this stunning passage begins with praise, ends with praise, and is infused with praise. There's another common thread that weaves its way through this passage, namely, we are chosen, adopted, and God's possession.

1. Read Ephesians 1:3-14. What key phrases keep appearing in this passage? What does each one reveal about what Paul wants us to know?

Ephesus was one of seven urban centers located near the Mediterranean Sea. Its location made it a hub for agriculture, industry, and trade. This prosperous city was known for its wide streets, huge buildings, and private homes built to impress visitors. It's worth noting that in writing to this affluent region, Paul doesn't emphasize financial blessings, rather he grounds believers in their spiritual blessings.

2. How many times does the word "in" appear in this passage? What does the frequency of "in" reveal about what Paul is trying to emphasize? What does this passage reveal about the source of our spiritual blessing?

In this opening chapter, Paul celebrates and exalts Christ and his work. Throughout Ephesians, Paul will continue to emphasize Jesus as the exalted one whose headship rules over the cosmos, creation, and the church.

3. Fill in the chart below by listing the blessings Paul names. Then place a star by the ones you need to experience more of right now.

EPHESIANS	SPIRITUAL BLESSING FOR YOUR LIFE
1:3	
1:4	
1:5	
1:6	
1:7	
1:9	
1:11–12	
1:13–14	

4. What's the purpose of these abundant blessings? (Hint: Ephesians 1:5-6, 10, 12, 14)

Romans sealed their scrolls six to seven times with soft wax over the edges of the parchment to ensure no one tampered with the contents without authorization. To be

means you are wholly his.

5. On the continuum below, how often do you struggle with inferiority, failure, or rejection? How does this passage speak truth into those false beliefs?

I often struggle with feelings of inferiority, failure, or rejection.

I never struggle with feelings of inferiority, failure, or rejection.

6. Read Ephesians 1:3-14 aloud again. As you do, replace "us" and "you" with your name. How does reading this passage as if it's written to you impact the way you hear it? How does knowing you have these holy provisions help you face life's hardships?

7. Who do you know who needs to be reminded of their spiritual blessings in Christ? Take a moment to reach out with an email, text, or phone call to remind them of just how much they are loved by God and you.

DAY 3
Ephesians 1:15–23

After recognizing the breadth of our spiritual blessings in Christ, Paul transitions to offer thanksgiving and prayer for the saints.

1. Read Ephesians 1:15-16. Which comes more easily to you—praise or prayer? Why?

2. Read Ephesians 1:17-19. What does Paul specifically pray that the Ephesians would come to know more deeply? Fill in the chart below.

EPHESIANS	PAUL'S PRAYER REQUESTS
1:17	
1:18	
1:19	
1:20	

"Eyes of your heart" refer to the **center** of one's being, the seat of one's mental, physical, and spiritual life.

3. Reflecting on the chart above, which entries do you tend to know more of in head knowledge and which do you tend to know more of in heart knowledge? Which of these do you most need to have the "eyes of your heart" opened to (vs. 18)?

4. Read Romans 8:15-17 and 1 Peter 1:3-6. What do these passages reveal about the glorious inheritance God has for us?

The church at Ephesus was located in a coastal region known as Asia's Supreme Metropolis. The city boasted one of the wonders of the ancient world, a temple for the "bee" goddess known as Artemis or Diana. Thousands of priests and priestesses worshiped and practiced cult prostitution in the city.

5. Read Ephesians 1:20-23. Why do you think the church of Ephesus needed to hear that all rulers, authorities, power, and dominions were under Jesus' control? In what area of your life do you most need to cling to this truth?

6. Where do you feel out of control in your life? How can you commit this area to the lordship of Christ?

7. Reflect on the hope-filled words of Ephesians 1:15-23. Who are three people you could send this passage to today in order to encourage them?

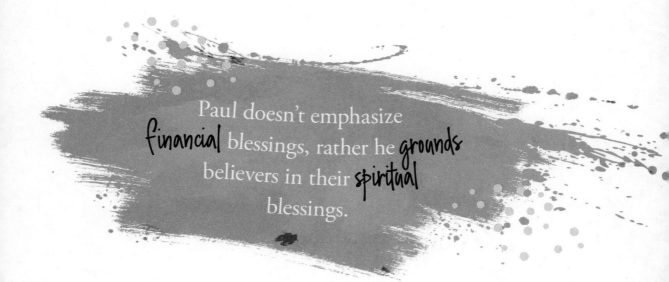

Paul doesn't emphasize *financial* blessings, rather he *grounds* believers in their *spiritual* blessings.

As you reflect on your personal study
of Ephesians 1, what are the beautiful words
the Holy Spirit has been highlighting to you
through this time? Write or draw them
in the space below.

ALIVE
IN
CHRIST

Ephesians

Opening Group Activity [10-15 MINUTES]

What you'll need:

▶ Sheet of blank paper for each person

▶ Pens, markers, and/or watercolors

1. Each participant is invited to use the paper and drawing/writing tools to create two pictures (in words or images). One should be of your life before Christ and one should be of your life after encountering Christ.

2. Discuss the following questions:

   • How was your life different before encountering Christ compared to after?

   • What are you most thankful for in the work Jesus has done in your life?

Session Two Video [21 MINUTES]

NOTES: *As you watch, take notes on anything that stands out to you.*

 Our transgressions and our sins don't just make us spiritually sick or badly injured, they make us completely dead.

 Sometimes I want to do what's good, but I just do what's bad, too.

What made you reflect? What

surprised you?

What caught your attention?

That word sin in the original language describes missing the mark in our lives.

Sometimes when we've been believers for a while, we're tempted to forget the pit that God pulled us out of.

If we want to walk with our heads held high, we also need to realize we've been revived, made alive again, with Christ.

If our salvation was dependent upon any work of our own, we would certainly boast about it, brag about it, or post about it.

Our situation was dire, but his gift is divine.

What caught your attention? What surprised you? What made you reflect?

EPHESIANS 2

Group Discussion Questions [30-45 MINUTES]

1. Lori says,

   ## "Many of us are going through life without much life going through us."

   Where in your life do you feel most alive? What's an area where you feel low-energy, numb, or lifeless? (Examples: work, parenting, a particular relationship, etc.) What has sapped your energy?

2. Read Ephesians 2:4-7. On a scale of 1 to 10, how alive in Christ are you right now? What spiritual practices or friendships jolt your aliveness in Christ? What prevents you from engaging in these more?

3. Lori tells the funny story of her son, Ethan, flushing random items down the toilet to illustrate the idea that sometimes we all do things that we know we shouldn't do. Which of the following are most tempting for you right now? Why? What encouragement do you find in Hebrews 2:17-18?

   - Being passive aggressive
   - Taking something that isn't yours
   - Responding in anger
   - Cutting corners
   - Lacking patience
   - Being resentful

   - Holding a grudge
   - Unleashing on social media
   - Beating yourself up
   - Crossing a boundary you've set
   - Numbing through indulgence
   - Other

4. Read Ephesians 2:8. Lori teaches that when we've been believers for a while, we're tempted to forget the pit that God pulled us out of. We can look at others, either much earlier in their journey with Christ or still dead in their sins, and have a hypercritical or judgmental attitude toward them. When are you most tempted to fall into a critical or

judgmental attitude toward someone? Why is it essential to remember what you've been redeemed from and that salvation is a gift?

5. Which of the following are you most likely to believe can save you other than Christ? Why is this your go-to? What's a healthier go-to replacement?

- Perfectionism
- Hard work
- Juicy bank account
- Big promotion
- Best friend
- Large insurance policy

- Successful kids
- Significant other
- Perfect body
- Miracle cure
- Busyness
- Other

6. Read Ephesians 2:10. Paul notes that we aren't just saved from something, we're saved for something. What good work do you sense God nudging you to do in this season? Is anything stopping you from responding wholeheartedly? If so, describe. How can friends or other members of this study group help encourage you in this area?

Close in Prayer

Consider the following prompts as you pray together for:

▶ Remembrance of all Christ has done in your life

▶ Abundant grace for all who are in a different place in their journey

▶ Awareness of the good works God has for you to do now

Preparation

To prepare for the next group session:

1. Read Ephesians 3.

2. Tackle the three days of the Session Two Personal Study.

3. Memorize this week's passage using the Beautiful Word Scripture memory coloring page. As a bonus, look up the Scripture memory passage in different translations and take note of the variations.

4. If you've agreed to bring something for the next session's Opening Group Activity, get it ready.

"But because of his great love for us, God, who is rich in mercy, made us alive with Christ even when we were dead in transgressions — it is by grace you have been saved."

—Ephesians 2:4-5

PERSONAL
STUDY TIME

DIGGING INTO THE

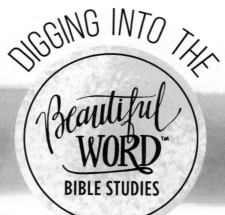

Beautiful
WORD™
BIBLE STUDIES

Ephesians
ALIVE IN CHRIST

DAY 1
Ephesians 2:1–10

After laying the foundation in the first chapter of the abundant blessings we have in Christ, Paul now shifts to tell us of the transformation that God is doing within us. And it's powerful!

1. Read Ephesians 2:1-5. What did God do with those who were unable to save and redeem themselves? What does this reveal about the character of God?

2. Fill in the chart below. List three areas of your life where you've experienced transformation because of Christ's work in your life and three areas where you long to experience transformation.

HAVE EXPERIENCED CHRIST'S TRANSFORMATION	LONG TO EXPERIENCE CHRIST'S TRANSFORMATION

The word Paul uses here in verse one for "transgressions" means to go beyond or overstep a limit or boundary. It gets to the idea of being a rebel, to know what you are supposed to do, but then choose not to do it—to understand the boundary that's been set, but willingly step across that limit.

3. What's an area of your life where you're struggling with doing what you know you shouldn't do? How can you gain strength and grace in this area with Christ?

4. Read Ephesians 2:6-7. In the square below, draw a picture of what's described in this passage.

The word  "handiwork"

(v.10) is derived from the Greek word  poiema, which is where we get the word poem

You are literally God's masterpiece poem to the world.

5. Read Ephesians 2:7-8. What's the most difficult part of grace for you?

6. How can you be a conduit of God's grace to someone else today?

7. Read Ephesians 2:10. On the continuum below, mark which best describes you. What are some of the good works God has prepared for you that you're doing right now?

I tend to live as if
I'm saved *by* good works.

I tend to live as if
I'm saved *for* good works.

DAY 2
Ephesians 2:11–18

Paul speaks to the Gentiles, those of non-Jewish descent, and reminds them of their spiritual condition before knowing Christ. They are called "uncircumcised." Physically, this describes males who had not had the foreskin of their manhood removed. But in antiquity, Jews who called Gentiles "uncircumcised" meant it as a term of disdain.

1. Read Ephesians 2:11-12. The only command Paul gives in this chapter is to "remember." What does Paul call us to remember? Make a list in the space below. Which of these is easiest for you to forget?

   • ....
   • ....
   • ....
   • ....
   • ....

2. Why do you think Paul is so keen on wanting us to remember who we are before and after encountering Christ?

In the Old Testament sacrificial system, God required the shedding of blood for forgiveness.

3. Read Ephesians 2:13 and Hebrews 9:14. What does the blood of Christ accomplish?

This is my blood of the covenant, which is poured out for many for the forgiveness of sins.

MATTHEW 26:28

PEACE in the Hebrew is *shalom.* It speaks of a holistic wellness, wholeness, and well-being.

Paul reminds us that through Jesus, Jews and Gentiles are brought together. Paul uses the word "peace" seven times in Ephesians and emphasizes the theme in this section.

4. Read Ephesians 2:14-18. What does Paul mean when he says, "Christ is our peace?" How have you experienced the "Prince of Peace" (Isaiah 9:6) this week?

5. What do believers living in peace regardless of circumstances communicate to the world?

6. Why do you think Christians struggle to live at peace with one another? Which of the following do you allow to create tension in your relationship with other believers? Place a star by each one.

.... Political differences   .... Theological differences
.... Racial differences   .... Language differences
.... Socio-economic differences   .... Cultural differences
.... Denominational differences   .... Other

7. Who is someone of faith you're struggling to live in peace with right now? What can you do to bring healing to the relationship?

DAY 3
Ephesians 2:19–22

While the second chapter of Ephesians opens by addressing separation and alienation from God, the chapter closes by highlighting the unity and holy connection God intends among believers. As Jews and Gentiles are brought together in Christ, the result is a flourishing church inhabited by God and accomplishing his purposes.

1. Read Ephesians 2:19-22. What is the final outcome of Jesus bringing together Jews and Gentiles?

2. How does this passage compel you to break down barriers between believers? Between you and others?

So this is what the Sovereign Lord says, "See, I lay a stone in Zion, a tested stone, a precious corner- stone for a sure founda- tion; the one who relies on it will never be stricken with panic."

Isaiah 28:16

3. What does God use to give you a new fellowship, a new family, and a new foundation?

4. Why does it matter that Jesus is the cornerstone of the church? What happens to a group of believers if they build their foundation on anything other than Christ?

5. Ephesians 2:1-10 and 2:11-18 are connected by the word "therefore." How do these two passages relate?

6. Ephesians 2:11-18 and 19-22 are connected by the word "consequently." How do these two passages relate?

7. Reflecting on the entire chapter, sum up Paul's message in one sentence. How does this message challenge you today?

As *Jews* and *Gentiles* are *brought together* in *Christ*, the result is a *flourishing* church inhabited by God and accomplishing *his* purposes.

As you reflect on your personal study of Ephesians 2, what are the beautiful words the Holy Spirit has been highlighting to you through this time? Write or draw them in the space below.

SESSION
3

EMPOWERED
BY
PRAYER

Ephesians

Opening Group Activity [10-15 MINUTES]

What you'll need:

- ▶ Sticky notes
- ▶ Pens
- ▶ A nearby wall, window, or flat surface

1. Give participants 3 to 5 sticky notes each and invite them to write a prayer request on each one.

2. Invite members to place their sticky note prayers on a nearby wall, window, or flat surface in such a way that together all the sticky notes form the shape of a cross.

3. Discuss the following questions:

   - What prayer request is pressing on your heart the most right now? Why?
   - What does your prayer life look like during the week?
   - What tempts you to give up on praying? What inspires you to pray more?

Session Three Video [22 MINUTES]

NOTES: *As you watch, take notes on anything that stands out to you.*

 If you want to walk with your head held high, you must first bow it in prayer.

 Bended knees is a physical posture that represents the position of our hearts—submitting to the will and purpose of God.

What caught your attention? What surprised you? What made you reflect? Wha

Prayer empowers by filling us with strength and power.

Another way to be empowered through prayer is to realize that Christ finds his home in our hearts.

Jesus makes his personal residency in you.

We're empowered by prayer when we fully understand God's love for us.

When we take into account the full measure of God's love—its length, width, height and depth—we realize that nothing and no one falls outside of the bounds of his love.

God just wants you home.

Group Discussion Questions (30-45 MINUTES)

1. Lori says,

   "**Nothing** drives me to my knees faster than my kids!"

   What in your life drives you to your knees the fastest?

2. Read Ephesians 3:16. Have you ever experienced this strengthening? If so, describe that experience.

3. It's been said that prayer doesn't change God but it changes us. How would you describe your prayer life right now? What barriers prevent you from having a more vibrant prayer life? What practices help you pray? (Ex. silence, Scripture, etc.)

4. Lori teaches,

   "Jesus wants to **dwell** in you, to be at home in you. He wants to be able to **access** every room, every closet, and every **junk** drawer you'd **never** show your guests."

   Which areas of your life do you try to hide or hold back from God by not talking to him about it? Where do you most need God to do a spiritual renovation in your heart?

5. Read Ephesians 3:17-18. In what specific ways has God's love healed you? In what situations do you most often sense God's love flowing through you?

6. What spiritual practices or activities help you experience God's love? Why is it important to experience God's love on a regular basis? What is standing in the way of giving yourself wholly and fully to God's love?

If you want to walk with your *head held high,* you must first *bow* it in prayer.

Close in Prayer

Consider the following prompts as you pray together for:

▸ The prayer requests from the opening activity

▸ A renewed desire to pray

▸ Opportunities to experience the relentless love of God

Preparation

1. Read Ephesians 4.

2. Tackle the three days of Session Three Personal Study.

3. Memorize this week's passage using the Beautiful Word Scripture memory coloring page. As a bonus, look up the Scripture memory passage in different translations and take note of the variations.

4. If you agreed to bring something for the next session's Opening Group Activity, make sure to have it ready.

"And I pray that *you*, being *rooted* and *established* in *love*, may have *power*, *together* with all the Lord's *holy* people, to grasp how *wide* and *long* and *high* and *deep* is the *love* of *Christ*..."

—Ephesians 3:17-18

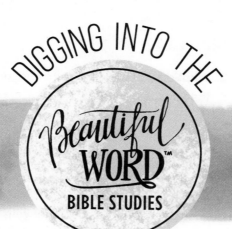

PERSONAL STUDY TIME

DIGGING INTO THE

Beautiful WORD™
BIBLE STUDIES

Ephesians

EMPOWERED BY PRAYER

DAY 1
Ephesians 3:1-6

Nero was a Roman emperor who ruled from 54 to 68AD famed for tyranny, abuse, and extravagance. His cruelty, compulsive nature, and corruption made him a dreaded leader.

After exploring how we are made alive in Christ and how Jews and Gentiles are brought into unity in Christ, Paul now returns to prayer as he did in the opening chapter. But in this third chapter, he interrupts himself to explore his current condition as a prisoner and his personal commission as God's messenger of salvation and reconciliation.

1. **Read Ephesians 3:1. Though Paul is in prison under Nero, who does he identify himself as a prisoner of? Why do you think he describes himself this way?**

2. **What do you find yourself imprisoned or enslaved by other than Jesus Christ?**

Paul had a remarkable encounter with God on the Road to Damascus. This transformed Paul from someone who persecuted Christians to someone who became one.

3. **Read Ephesians 3:2-3 and Acts 22:6-21. How did Paul encounter God's grace? What about this encounter surprises you?**

4. Read 2 Corinthians 12:9. Describe a time when you encountered God's grace. Why does experiencing God's grace sometimes include hardship, conflict, or weakness?

5. Read Ephesians 3:4-6. What is the mystery that God is revealing?

6. Look up the following passages. What does each one reveal about the mysteries or secrets revealed by God?

   ● Job 11:7:

   ● Luke 8:10:

   ● 1 Corinthians 2:7:

   ● Colossians 2:2:

7. In the space below, write a prayer of thanks for the ways that God has made himself known to you.

In Greek, the word "mystery" doesn't describe a personal secret, but rather a divine truth revealed by God that belongs to the entire church.

The Greek word

anexichniaston

(verse 8) only occurs **twice** in the New Testament and can be translated "unsearchable" or "boundless" in describing the riches in Christ. It can mean incomprehensible or impossible to fathom.

DAY 2
Ephesians 3:7–13

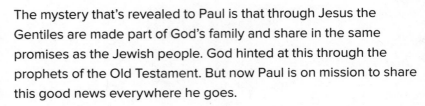

The mystery that's revealed to Paul is that through Jesus the Gentiles are made part of God's family and share in the same promises as the Jewish people. God hinted at this through the prophets of the Old Testament. But now Paul is on mission to share this good news everywhere he goes.

1. Read Ephesians 3:7-9. What mission is Paul compelled to fulfill? What is the fuel that propels Paul to accomplish this mission? (v. 7) What does it look like for you to tap into grace in your daily life?

2. Based on Ephesians 3:8, how would you complete the following sentence:

   Although I am less than the least of all the Lord's people, this grace was given me:

   ....

   ....

   ....

Paul suggests that everyone in the heavenly realms—even God's enemies—are put on notice that through Christ salvation is available to all people.

3. Read Ephesians 3:10-11. On the continuum below, mark how easy it is for you to share your faith. Take a moment to pray for the opportunity to share your faith with someone this week.

It's easy and natural for me to share my faith.

I struggle to share my faith.

Despite the clarity of Paul's mission, he often encountered hostility, adversity and suffering.

4. Read Ephesians 3:12. Does anything hold you back from approaching God in the fullness of freedom and confidence? If so, describe.

5. Read Ephesians 3:13 and Acts 21:27-36. What was the response to Paul's message?

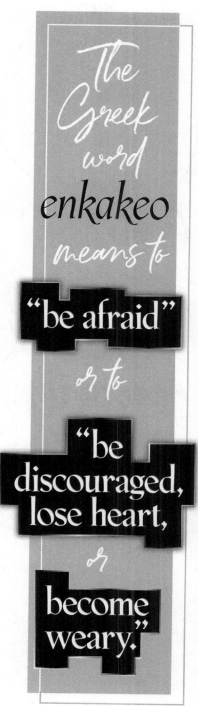

The Greek word *enkakeo* means to "be afraid" or to "be discouraged, lose heart, or become weary."

Throughout Paul's letters, he often links glory and riches. Glory describes *God's splendor,* while riches are the basis of *God's generosity.* You'll find these linked in **Romans 9:23, Philippians 4:19, Colossians 1:27, and more.**

6. When you feel compelled by God to do something or share your faith, do you tend to expect that it will go well or that you'll encounter adversity? Where are you struggling with discouragement most right now? Why do you think Paul's encouragement to not become discouraged is so important?

DAY 3
Ephesians 3:14–21

After beginning the chapter in prayer, Paul now returns to his prayer again. He begins by saying, "For this reason, I kneel before the Father..." (v. 14). For those in the early church, standing was the predominant position of prayer, though kneeling happened, too. The physical posture isn't as important as the posture of the heart.

Throughout this section, Paul's words are marked by an eloquence and beauty that's grand and inspiring. It challenges believers to know the fullness of Christ and his love and to walk in the fullness of faith.

1. Read Ephesians 3:14-19. What does Paul specifically pray for in this passage?

2. Which element of this prayer do you need most desperately in your life right now? Why?

3. What would your life look like without God's love? What do the dimensions of God's love communicate about how much God wants you to experience it?

4. Is there anything about God's love that scares you or makes you want to withdraw? If so, describe. Where do you think that resistance to God's love came from?

5. Read Ephesians 3:20. Paul says that God can do "immeasurably more" than we ask for or imagine. On the continuum below, mark how easy it is for you to pray and believe God for immeasurably more.

I struggle to ask and believe God for the immeasurably more.

It's easy to ask and believe God for the immeasurably more.

When Paul prays that we "may have power, together with all the Lord's holy people" (v. 18) to grasp the expansiveness of God's *love*, it suggests that this relentless divine affection is *available* to all believers and that grasping this love happens through being part of a community of saints.

6. In what areas of your life do you tend to ask or imagine God for immeasurably less than he is capable of? Why do you think you place limits on God?

7. Identify the one area of your life where you need God to do immeasurably more. Now write a prayer asking for God to do more than you ever thought possible in the space below.

....

....

....

....

....

For those in the early church, *standing* was the predominant position of prayer, though *kneeling* happened, too. The physical posture isn't as important as the *posture* of the *heart*.

As you reflect on your personal study of Ephesians 3, what are the beautiful words that the Holy Spirit has been highlighting to you through this time? Write or draw them in the space below.

SESSION
4

LIVE
WORTHY

Ephesians

Opening Group Activity [10-15 MINUTES]

What you'll need:

▶ Small slips of paper or sticky notes

▶ Pen

▶ Bowl

1. Before the gathering, write one of the following words/phrases on a slip of paper until all of them have been used: Worthy. Loved. Beautiful. Strong. Perfect. God's vessel. Forgiven. Stunning. Sealed by God. Remarkable. Holy. Treasure. Free. Accepted. Jesus' friend. God's child. Redeemed. Chosen. Anointed. Made new. Fruitful. Powerful. Beloved. Triumphant. Radiant. Wonderfully made. God's instrument. Priceless. Victorious.

2. Invite members to draw one slip of paper and pass the bowl around the group until all the members have two or more slips of paper. You may need to create duplicates based on the size of your group.

3. Discuss the following questions:

   • Reflecting on the slips of paper you have, which one is easiest for you to believe and live out? Which is hardest? Why?

   • How does knowing who you are in Christ help you to walk with your head held high?

Session Four Video [22 MINUTES]

NOTES: *As you watch, take notes on anything that stands out to you.*

 Even if you feel unqualified, unworthy, or unprepared, God has given you a calling, a ministry.

 We live worthy because he already loves us.

What caught your attention? What surprised you? What made you reflect? Wh

True humility isn't putting yourself down but rather lifting up God and others.

 Paul doesn't just say to be humble, he also says we need to be gentle.

 Gentleness comes from knowing that God's plan is sovereign.

 Patience is sticking it out and enduring difficult circumstances.

 If we want to live worthy, we need to also remember that God's kingdom is worthy.

 God's looking for people who believe his name is worthy.

 The most powerful word we can declare over our situations is: "Jesus, Jesus, Jesus, Jesus, Jesus, Jesus, Jesus."

Group Discussion Questions [30-45 MINUTES]

1. How would you describe your calling, ministry, or area of influence that God is using you in right now? How does your role help build the larger body of Christ?

2. In what area of your life do you feel most unworthy? Where do you tend to turn for your sense of worth other than God? How does that fulfill you? How does that leave you feeling empty?

3. When you sense God calling you to step out in obedience, which do you tend to wrestle with most: feeling unqualified, unworthy, or unprepared? Explain. What comfort do you find in knowing God is simply inviting you into what he's already doing?

4. Lori asks,

"What do you do when the calling is weighty? When that ministry doesn't feel wonderful? When joining God in what he's doing seems overwhelming?" What is your response?

5. Read Ephesians 4:2-3. What does Paul specifically call us to in order to walk worthy? Which one comes most naturally to you? Which one do you tend to struggle with most? Why?

6. Lori teaches,

"The most powerful word we can declare over our situations is: "Jesus, Jesus, Jesus, Jesus, Jesus, Jesus, Jesus."

Where in your life do you most need to declare this right now?

Walking *worthy* is *not* about what we are doing, it's about *how* we are *living.*

Close in Prayer

Consider the following prompts as you pray together for:

▶ The courage to walk worthy in Christ

▶ Opportunities to see God's name, plan, timing, and kingdom as worthy

▶ Moments to practice gentleness, patience, and grace with others

Preparation

To prepare for the next group session:

1. Read Ephesians 5.

2. Tackle the three days of Session Four Personal Study.

3. Memorize this week's passage using the Beautiful Word Scripture memory coloring page. As a bonus, look up the Scripture memory passage in different translations and take note of the variations.

4. If you've agreed to bring something for the next session's Opening Group Activity, get it ready.

"As a prisoner for the Lord, then, I urge you to live a life worthy of the calling you have received."

—Ephesians 4:1

PERSONAL STUDY TIME

DIGGING INTO THE

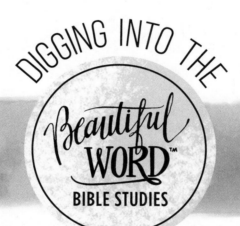

Beautiful
WORD™
BIBLE STUDIES

Ephesians
LIVE WORTHY

> That all of them may be one, Father, just as you are in me and I am in you. May they also be in us so that the world may believe that you have sent me.
>
> John 17:21

DAY 1
Ephesians 4:1-6

While the first half of Ephesians calls us to the fullness of who we are in Christ, the second half of the letter explains how we are to live as Christians. This transition is marked by the words, "I urge you" (v.1). Paul builds on many of the themes that appeared in the first three chapters including the call to love, unity, and faithfulness. He gets specific and practical when it comes to what we must do in order to walk with our heads held high.

1. Read Ephesians 4:1-2 and 1 John 1:7. How are the source of your worth and walking worthy connected? Can you walk worthy without knowing your worth? Why or why not?

Some translations of verse 1 urge us to "walk in a manner worthy of the calling" (NASB).

2. Look up the following passages. What does each one reveal about living and walking worthy?

SCRIPTURE	CHARACTERISTICS OF WALKING WORTHY
Romans 6:13	
2 Corinthians 5:7	

SCRIPTURE	CHARACTERISTICS OF WALKING WORTHY
Galatians **5:16**	
1 John **1:7**	

3. Read Ephesians 4:3-6. Why do you think Paul urges us to make every effort to keep unity through the bond of peace?

In Ephesians, Paul emphasizes the title of "Father" when he speaks of God. This appears in every chapter of the book including in 4:6.

4. Describe a time when disunity entered a group of believers. What did it look like? What was the result?

5. Paul uses the word "one" seven times in this passage. Make a list of everything Paul describes as "one." Which do you believe the Christians you know personally are struggling with most? Which are you struggling with most?

1. ....

2. ....

3. ....

4. ....

5. ....

6. ....

7. ....

6. What's the difference between unity and uniformity? When have you succumbed to uniformity? What was the result?

7. What can you do to promote unity among believers you know?

DAY 2
Ephesians 4:7–16

At this point in the fourth chapter of Ephesians, Paul makes a subtle but significant shift. He moves from writing to "you" to writing to "us". Not only does this literary turn signal show that he's more closely linked with his readers, but it communicates the idea that we are all in this together and unity among believers is crucial.

1. **Read Ephesians 4:7.** What is the gift of grace you sense God has given you? How have you been using your gift of grace to bring healing and hope to others?

2. **Read Ephesians 4:8-10.** Christ deserves gifts and honor for his sacrifice, yet he chooses to be a generous giver. What does this reveal about the character of God? How he sees you?

3. **Read Ephesians 4:11.** What does this passage reveal about the diversity of giftings Christ gives?

4. Have you ever looked at someone else's calling, ministry, position, or role and thought, "I wish that was me"? If so, describe.

When you ascended on high, you took many captives; you received gifts from people, even from the rebellious— that you, Lord God, might dwell there.

PSALM 68:18

Paul notes that GOD GIVES every person gracious gifts, not just leaders (v. 7). For the church to flourish, God intends for every person to use their giftings.

5. How does trying to be someone you're not short-circuit the work Jesus is doing in and through you?

6. Read Ephesians 4:12-13. What is the purpose of the diversity of giftings and callings according to this passage?

Paul draws on imagery of the human body to communicate how much we need each other (v. 16). Just as bones, ligaments, muscles, and organs work together, so too, believers are deeply interconnected with each other. We cannot fulfill our individual roles or become fully mature without working together.

7. Read Romans 12:10-16. What does this passage reveal about how much we need each other? What does this passage reveal about the dangers of living a solitary faith? What steps do you need to take to become more interconnected with other believers?

DAY 3
Ephesians 4:17-32

After a clarion call to maturity and unity, Paul now becomes explicit about the choices we make and what we are to do and not do. Through Christ, we receive the grace to change, but we must make the decision and act on it. Paul draws on imagery as he instructs us on what to put off and put on as followers of Jesus

1. Read Ephesians 4:17-19. When have you seen one small sin grow into something much larger in someone else's life? How have you seen the tentacles of sin grow in your life?

2. Read Ephesians 4:20-24. What is Christ making new in you according to this passage?

3. Where are you still clinging to your old life, way of thinking, or behavior? What steps can you take now to break free from them?

Paul instructs, "In your anger do not sin" (v. 26).

Notice he leaves space for righteous anger—whether toward injustice or falsehood. Jesus was *angry* at the temple when he saw the abuses taking place.

See Matthew 21:12-17.

4. **Read Ephesians 4:25-28. Rank the following in order of which you struggle with most. Place a 1 by your biggest struggle and a 4 by the least.**

.... Being completely honest with your words

.... Reacting in anger or a hot temper

.... Taking something from others

.... Being lazy or feeling entitled

How do each of these behaviors or attitudes undermine unity and healthy relationships? Why do you think we're told to not do these things?

1. ....
....

2. ....
....

3. ....
....

4. ....
....

5. **Read Ephesians 4:29-32. In the chart on the next page, write out what Paul tells us to avoid and what we're instructed to do. If you do what Paul instructs, how are these an antidote to unbecoming behavior?**

PAUL'S INSTRUCTION OF WHAT NOT TO DO	PAUL'S INSTRUCTION OF WHAT TO DO

6. How does remembering that Christ forgave you empower you to forgive others?

7. How many times does Paul address the issue of the words we speak in this passage? How careful are you with your words? Who are three people you can speak living words to today?

The Greek word for "unwholesome", sapos, refers to something of poor quality to the point of causing harm.

As you reflect on your personal study of Ephesians 4, what are the beautiful words the Holy Spirit has been highlighting to you through this time? Write or draw them in the space below.

WALK

IN

LIGHT

Ephesians

Opening Group Activity [10-15 MINUTES]

What you'll need:

▶ A music player (such as a smart phone) with a downloaded playlist so you are ready to play a song that speaks of the Holy Spirit such as "Spirit of the Living God," "Let the Heavens Open," or "Breathe on Me, Breath of God."

1. Invite one volunteer to read Ephesians 5:18-19.

2. Invite everyone in the group to listen or sing along to the selected song. You may even want to have the words of your selection printed out or provide a link to the lyrics for everyone.

3. Discuss the following questions:

▶ How often do you do what Paul instructs in Ephesians 5:18-19?

▶ Why is this practice important for believers to do together?

▶ What steps can you take to incorporate this practice into your life and relationships?

Session Five Video [22 MINUTES]

NOTES: *As you watch, take notes on anything that stands out to you.*

 In the darkness, we chased sin. Our deeds were fruitless. We were disobedient and secretive.

 Jesus shed light on the dark places so we can share light in the dark places.

What made you reflect? Wh

What surprised you?

What caught your attention?

Righteousness is a rightness of character that is rooted in the rightness of God.

 We are the walking demonstrations of the truth of the Bible. We are the living profession of the Truth, who is Jesus.

 We can go through life without much life going through us.

 Every day we need to ask God to fill us with his Spirit—that the Holy Spirit will guide us and direct us.

Group Discussion Questions (30-45 MINUTES)

1. Read Ephesians 5:8-13. Why do you think staying in the darkness is sometimes preferable to experiencing the light? How do you tend to respond to the light of God illuminating your darkest area? Do you tend to be excited, hesitant, scared, or have another response? Explain.

2. What is the result of God's light doing its work in our lives? Write a one-sentence prayer asking God to expose your darkness. Consider praying this aloud with the group.

3. Lori teaches,

"Many of us are living a drowsy life of faith. We've been lulled back to sleep in a stagnant spiritual life. We drift into autopilot in our relationship with Jesus."

Where in your life is this true of you? Where do you most need to wake up?

4. On a scale of 1 to 10, how would you describe yourself as a procrastinator? Where are you most tempted to practice spiritual procrastination? What are the long-term effects of spiritual procrastination in your relationship with God?

5. Read John 14:26, Romans 8:26-27, and 1 Corinthians 2:10-11. What role does the Holy Spirit play in your everyday life? How can you live a more Spirit-filled life?

6. What are the "this is now" opportunities available to you in your home and relationships? Where do you most need to declare and respond to God that "this is now?"

Close in Prayer

Consider the following prompts as you pray together for:

▶ God to illuminate every part of your life

▶ Awareness of any areas of spiritual procrastination

▶ Opportunities to live as if "This is now" in your relationship with Christ

Jesus shed light on the dark places so you can share light in the dark places.

Preparation

1. Read Ephesians 6.

2. Tackle the three days of Session Five Personal Study.

3. Memorize this week's passage using the Beautiful Word Scripture memory coloring page. As a bonus, look up the Scripture memory passage in different translations and take note of the variations.

4. If you've agreed to bring something for the next session's Opening Group Activity, get it ready.

"For you were once darkness, but now you are light in the Lord. Live as children of light."

—Ephesians 5:8

PERSONAL
STUDY TIME

DIGGING INTO THE

Beautiful
WORD™
BIBLE STUDIES

Ephesians
WALK IN LIGHT

When Paul uses the term *"fragrant offering"* (v. 2), he paints a picture of the scent of sacrifice that arose to God in the Old Testament and brought him pleasure.

See Exodus 29:18.

DAY 1
Ephesians 5:1–7

One of the ways we demonstrate family likeness is by being like the rest of our family. That's one of the reasons Paul encourages us to follow God's example and walk in the way of love demonstrated by Christ. In this fifth chapter, Paul continues his listings of do's and don'ts for believers who want to be like their Heavenly Father.

1. **Read Ephesians 5:1-2. What does it look like for you to walk in the way of love?**

2. **What's the biggest sacrifice you are making because of your faith night now?**

3. **Is there anything Christ has called you to let go of that you're still holding on to? If so, describe. What steps do you need to take to pry yourself free?**

4. Read Ephesians 5:3-5. In the chart below, write out what Paul instructs us to avoid and what we're instructed to do. Why do you think Paul says there should not even be a hint of these things?

PAUL'S INSTRUCTION OF WHAT NOT TO DO	PAUL'S INSTRUCTION OF WHAT TO DO

5. Read Ephesians 5:5. How are these present in your life through your thoughts, attitudes, actions, or behaviors?

Immoral:

Impure:

Greed:

6. What do you need to do to repent, change your mind, and break free from these?

7. Read Ephesians 5:6-7. Is there anyone in your life who is influencing you toward unhealthy, self-sabotaging, or ungodly behavior? What healthy boundaries do you need to establish in that relationship so you can walk in health, wholeness, and holiness?

DAY 2
Ephesians 5:8-20

Throughout the New Testament, John often referred to the themes of light and darkness (John 1:5, 8:12, 9:15, 12:35-36; 1 John 1:5-7). Here Paul draws on the imagery of light and darkness to highlight who we are to become in Christ.

1. Read Ephesians 5:8-10. What does it look like for you to live as a child of light? Draw a picture in the space below. What is the fruit of being a child of light?

2. **How do you find out what is pleasing to the Lord? What do you think is most pleasing to the Lord in your life right now?**

Paul shouts for us to "Wake up!" with the promise that when we repent or change our ways, the light of Christ shines on us, in us, and through us. He draws on Isaiah 26:19 and Isaiah 60:1 to call us from death to life and darkness to light.

3. **Read Ephesians 5:11-16. Where do you sense the Holy Spirit is calling you to wake up and walk in the light?**

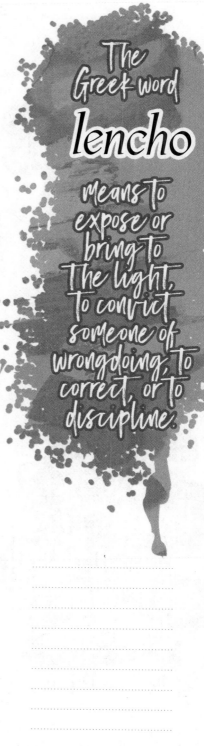

The Greek word **lencho** means to expose or bring to the light, to convict someone of wrongdoing, to correct, or to discipline.

4. **Read Ephesians 5:15-17. On the continuum below, mark how intentional you are about the way you live your life. What are some of the wisest decisions you've made in life? What are some of the most foolish? What does it look like for you to make the most of every opportunity?**

I'm not very
intentional
about how I
live my life.

I'm very
intentional
about how I
live my life.

Besides this, you know what time it is, how it is now the moment, for you to wake from sleep. For salvation is nearer to us now than when we became believers.

Romans 13:11 NRSV

5. Read Ephesians 5:18-20. Paul instructs us not to be drunk on wine, but in our modern day many other numbing devices are available. What do you tend to use to numb the pain in your life? How does numbing pain impair your ability to experience healing?

6. What role does praise, worship, and music play in your spiritual life? How can you become more intentional in your praise and worship?

7. Does gratitude play a role in your life? In the space below, make a list of ten things you're thankful to God for right now. How does practicing gratitude affect your emotions and outlook on life?

1. ....

2. ....

3. ....

4. ....

5. ....

6. ....

7. ....

8. ....

9. ....

10. ....

DAY 3
Ephesians 5:21–33

Paul shows how being filled to the brim with the Holy Spirit leads to mutual submission. The Greek word for submit, *hypotasso*, means to subject oneself to the needs of others so their welfare is of more importance. This generous love toward others is based in reverence for Jesus and an expression of his love to and through us.

1. Read Ephesians 5:21. Who does Paul encourage us to submit to? What makes it challenging for you to yield to someone else's needs and desires?

2. When you hear the word submit, what positive connotations come to mind? What negative connotations pop up? What has most influenced your attitude toward the word "submit?" If this word is negative to you, what could turn it into a positive?

When Paul instructs *husbands* to *love* their *wives* (v. 25), he uses the *Greek* word *agapao*, a kind of love that originates in God's love for humanity. Paul has used this agape love in describing *God's love for Jesus* (1:6), *God's love for his people* (1:4), and *Jesus' love for the church* (5:2). This command to love with abandon has been emphasized throughout Ephesians and continues here.

After addressing the relationship of Christians toward each other, Paul now turns toward husbands and wives.

3. Read Ephesians 5:22-30. In the chart below, fill out what wives and husbands are instructed to do. Place a star by any of the instructions that are most challenging for you.

PAUL'S INSTRUCTION FOR WIVES	PAUL'S INSTRUCTION FOR HUSBANDS

4. What do you think God's response is to a husband who uses this passage to take advantage of, abuse, or cause emotional/mental harm to his wife?

5. Read Ephesians 5:31-33. How does the instruction of how husbands treat their wives reveal Christ's love for the church?

6. What roles do love and respect play in a marriage? What roles do love and respect play in a church? How do a marriage and the church suffer without them?

7. Who are three couples you can reach out to today to encourage in their marriage?

In verse 31, Paul quotes **Genesis 2:24** suggesting that God invented marriage in the garden, in part, **to reveal Christ's love** for the church.

As you reflect on your personal study
of Ephesians 5, what are the beautiful words
the Holy Spirit has been highlighting to you
through this time? Write or draw them
in the space below.

SESSION 6

TAKE
YOUR
STAND

Ephesians

Opening Group Activity [10-15 MINUTES]

What you'll need:

▶ Each person to bring food to share

▶ Party balloons or fun decorations

1. Decorate the room with balloons, streamers, wildflowers, and anything you can find to create a festive atmosphere.

2. Enjoy laughing, talking, sharing, and catching up as you eat together.

3. Discuss the following:

   ● What have you enjoyed most about the book of Ephesians?

   ● What's one question from the homework or discussion that really challenged you or stuck with you?

Session Six Video [22 MINUTES]

NOTES: *As you watch, take notes on anything that stands out to you.*

 We can't make a stand hunched over and slumped under the weight of insecurity, shame, and fear. No! We take our stand, shoulders back, chin up, head held high.

 Sometimes you need to punch the devil in the face.

What caught your attention? What surprised you? What made you reflect? Wh

We need to stand firm in God's strength so we can stand up under life's challenges.

 The enemy doesn't stand a chance when you stand in God's strength.

 God's truth is what holds everything together.

 Faith gives us a sure defense against the fiery missiles thrown in our direction.

Just like athletes, when you put on a helmet it not only protects you, it also identifies you.

SCRIPTURE COVERED IN THIS SESSION:
EPHESIANS 6

Group Discussion Questions [30-45 MINUTES]

1. Describe a time when you were met with resistance, difficulties, or challenges and knew there were spiritual dynamics involved? How do you find a healthy balance between the extremes of looking for the devil under every bush and denying the existence of evil in the world?

2. Consider the following list. Which of the following are you in a battle for right now? How weary are you from the battle? What can you do to find your strength and refuel in Christ?

   _____ Emotions   _____ Mental health   _____ Physical health   _____ Finances

   _____ Marriage   _____ Children   _____ Family   _____ Hope

   _____ Fearlessness   _____ Peace   _____ Future   _____ Other

3. Read Ephesians 6:13-17. On a scale of 1 to 10, how much do you feel like you're in a spiritual battle right now? Which part of the armor of God do you need to put on most right now? Why?

4. Lori teaches,

   "**Temptation** is an arrow that can **burn** your resolve. **Doubt** is an arrow that can **burn** your confidence. **Fear** is an arrow that can **burn** your joy. **Insecurity** is an arrow that can **burn** your sense of purpose."

   Which of these fiery arrows of the enemy are you most susceptible to? Why? What helps you stand strong when you're under attack?

5. Reflecting on the discussion and notes from the previous sessions, how have you learned to walk with your head held high through the book of Ephesians? What are you most excited to share about God with others as a result of this study? What does it look like for you to walk with your head held high in everyday life?

6. How would you sum up the book of Ephesians in a few words? What's the most beautiful aspect of Ephesians to you? What's your biggest takeaway from this Beautiful Word study? How will you live your life differently because of this discovery?

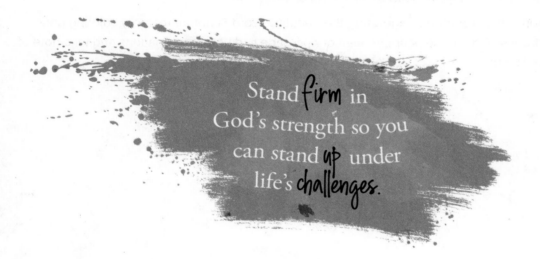

Stand *firm* in God's strength so you can stand *up* under life's *challenges.*

Close in Prayer

Consider the following prompts as you pray together for:

▶ Clarity for when we're fighting against spiritual powers

▶ Strength from God for the battles of life

▶ The full armor of God on each person

1. Read Ephesians 6.

2. Tackle the three days of Session Six Personal Study Time.

3. Memorize this week's passage using the Beautiful Word Scripture memory coloring page. As a bonus, look up the Scripture memory passage in different translations and take note of the variations.

"Be strong in the Lord and in his mighty power."

—Ephesians 6:10

PERSONAL
STUDY TIME

DIGGING INTO THE

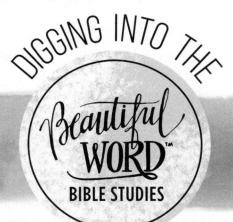

Beautiful
WORD™
BIBLE STUDIES

Ephesians
TAKE YOUR STAND

In Hebrew, the word honor, *kabed*, means "to be heavy or weighty" suggesting the one who is honored is worthy of respect and high value.

DAY 1
Ephesians 6:1-9

Paul challenges us to walk in love, walk in the light, and walk in wisdom. Now he calls us to walk in obedience. Yet his message is revolutionary and subversive to the culture he addresses. In antiquity, fathers had full legal rights over their children, and some used this authority to engage in harsh, abusive, or violent behavior. Some dads used their legal rights to sell their daughters into slavery. In this passage, Paul calls fathers to a higher standard, one that doesn't allow for any abuse.

1. Read Ephesians 6:1-4 and Deuteronomy 5:16. What promise is given to children who obey their parents? Do any of the other commandments contain a promise? If so, which ones?

2. How do you think God responds to parents who use this passage to abuse, exploit, or neglect their children? How does Paul oppose all forms of poor treatment of children in verse 4?

3. How does this passage apply to adult children caring for their aging parents?

4. What's one thing you can do today to honor and love your parents, even if they've passed away?

The word "exasperate" means to spark anger.

In the ancient world, some slave owners unleashed mental, emotional, and physical abuse on their slaves. They justified it as common treatment and even necessary. Paul writes subversively. First, he addresses slaves directly (something that was not done in antiquity, that was reserved for the elite superiors). Then he recognizes them as part of God's family. He gives them the dignity of their humanity.

5. Read Ephesians 6:5-9. When have you ever treated someone harshly because of your position or authority? How will you humble yourself and apologize?

6. What lessons can be drawn from this passage for business owners, bosses, and employees today? What in this passage speaks to your current employment or volunteer situation?

7. What are three ways you can demonstrate obedience to those who are in authority over you? What are three ways you can demonstrate compassion and kindness to those who are under your authority?

DAY 2
Ephesians 6:10-24

Paul concludes his letter with a final charge for believers to stand strong, head held high against the forces of spiritual darkness.

1. Read Ephesians 6:10-12. Describe a situation where you've thought you've been wrestling against flesh and blood but in light of this passage, you realize there might be a spiritual dynamic involved. How does this awareness shape your response to the situation?

2. **What do the following passages reveal about spiritual warfare?**

- John 10:10: ....

  ....

- 1 Corinthians 10:13: ....

  ....

- 2 Corinthians 10:4-5: ....

  ....

- 1 Peter 5:8-9: ....

  ....

- James 4:7: ....

  ....

- 2 Thessalonians 3:3: ....

  ....

3. **Read Ephesians 6:13-17. In the space below, draw a picture of the armor of God and then write down the function of each piece. Place a circle around all of the armor that's used for defense. Which of the pieces are meant for offensive roles?**

In verse 23, the Greek word for "brothers and sisters", adelphoi, refers to believers, both men and women, as part of God's family.

4. Which of the pieces of armor is hardest for you to wear on a consistent basis? Which is the easiest? What steps can you take to put on all the armor each day?

5. Read Ephesians 6:18-20. What practices spark a more vibrant prayer life in you? What prevents you from doing these more?

6. Read Ephesians 6:21-24. What does Paul give to the readers in the final two verses of the letter? How have these been appearing throughout Ephesians?

7. What's most encouraging to you in Ephesians 6? What's most challenging to you?

DAY 3
Your Beautiful Word

Review your notes and responses throughout this study guide. Place a star by those that stand out to you. Then respond to the following questions.

1. What's one thing you never knew about Ephesians that you know now? How has that knowledge impacted you?

2. What are three of the most important truths you learned from studying Ephesians?

3. After reviewing the six Beautiful Word coloring pages, which one stands out to you the most? Why?

4. What's one practical application from the study that you've put into practice? What's one practical application from the study that you still need to exercise?

5. What changes have you noticed in your attitudes, actions, and behaviors as a result of studying Ephesians?

6. How are you treating or responding to others differently as a result of this study?

7. How are you walking with your head held high as a result of this study?

As you reflect on your personal study of Ephesians 6, what are the beautiful words the Holy Spirit has been highlighting to you through this time? Write or draw them in the space below.

SESSION 1

"FOR HE **CHOSE** US IN HIM **BEFORE** THE CREATION OF THE WORLD TO BE **HOLY** AND **BLAMELESS** IN HIS SIGHT."

Ephesians 1:4

SESSION 2

"BUT BECAUSE OF HIS **GREAT LOVE** FOR US, GOD, WHO IS **RICH IN MERCY**, MADE US **ALIVE** WITH CHRIST EVEN WHEN WE WERE **DEAD** IN TRANSGRESSIONS— IT IS BY GRACE **YOU** HAVE BEEN **SAVED**."

Ephesians 2:4-5

SESSION 3

"AND I PRAY THAT **YOU**, BEING **ROOTED** AND ESTABLISHED IN **LOVE**, MAY HAVE **POWER**, TOGETHER WITH **ALL** THE LORD'S HOLY PEOPLE, TO GRASP HOW **WIDE** AND **LONG** AND **HIGH** AND **DEEP** IS THE **LOVE** OF CHRIST . . . ."

Ephesians 3:17-18

SESSION 4

"As a **PRISONER** for the LORD, then, I urge you to **LIVE** a life **WORTHY** of the **CALLING** you have received."

Ephesians 4:1

SESSION 5

"For **YOU** were once **DARKNESS**, but **NOW** you are **LIGHT** in the LORD. **LIVE** as children of **LIGHT**.'"

Ephesians 5:8

SESSION 6

" ...Be **STRONG** in the **LORD** and in his **MIGHTY POWER**.'"

Ephesians 6:10

ABOUT THE AUTHOR

Lori Wilhite serves alongside her husband Jud who is the Senior Pastor at Central Church in Las Vegas. Central currently has more than twenty-seven locations nationally and internationally including twelve locations inside prisons around the country.

She is the founder of Leading and Loving It which exists to equip and encourage women in leadership to love life in ministry. Lori believes in order to have healthy ministries, we must first be healthy women, healthy wives, and have healthy families. So, she is dedicated to encouraging the over 20,000 pastors' wives and women in leadership in the Leading and Loving It community through an annual conference, the JustONE online conference, leadership toolboxes, resource development and much more.

She is the author of *Rise Up!* and *My Name is Victorious*. Lori also co-authored *My Name is Victorious: Teen Edition* with her daughter and *Leading and Loving It: Encouragement for Pastors' Wives and Women in Leadership* with Brandi Wilson. Lori is the proud mom of two hilarious kids, Emma and Ethan. She loves laughing until her sides hurt with friends, reading novels cuddled up under cozy blankets on the couch, and crying during episodes of *Antiques Roadshow.*

Discover the Beauty of God's Word

The Beautiful Word™ Bible Study Series helps you connect God's Word to your daily life through vibrant video teaching, group discussion, and deep personal study that includes verse-by-verse reading, Scripture memory, coloring pages, and encouragement to receive your own beautiful Word from God.

In each study, a central theme—a beautiful word—threads throughout the book, helping you connect and apply each book of the Bible to your daily life today, and forever.

HarperChristianResources

IN THIS SERIES:

GALATIANS — Jada Edwards — Available Now

REVELATION — Margaret Feinberg — Available Now

EPHESIANS — Lori Wilhite — Available Now

ROMANS — Jada Edwards — Winter 2021

LUKE — Lisa Harper — Spring 2022

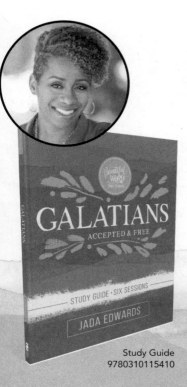

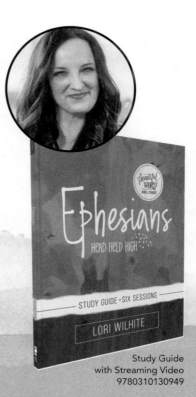

Study Guide
9780310115410

Study Guide
9780310122388

Study Guide
with Streaming Video
9780310130949

These Bible studies, along with Beautiful Word™ Bibles and
Bible Journals are available wherever books are sold.

H Harper*Christian*Resources

 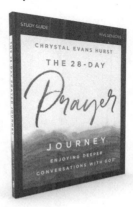

LEADING & LOVING IT

Committed to **equipping** + **encouraging** women leaders to love life in ministry.

Connect with Founder, Lori Wilhite and the
Leading and Loving It Community through

RE:TREAT
JUST**ONE** VIRTUAL CONFERENCE
EQUIP & ENCOURAGE TOOLBOXES
DEVOTIONS & RESOURCES
and much more.